This book belongs to:

____

Made in the USA
Las Vegas, NV
21 December 2021

39102846R00069